D1827121

THE

CASE

OF

OPPOSITION

STATED,

Between the

CRAFTSMAN

AND THE

PEOPLE.

Occasioned by his PAPER
of *December* the 4th, 1731.

LONDON:
Printed for J. ROBERTS, near the *Oxford
Arms* in *Warwick-Lane.* MDCCXXXI.

THE
CASE
OF
OPPOSITION
STATED, &c.

HE Paper before us is an APPEAL TO THE PUBLICK; it contains a Recapitulation of the Labours of the *Craftsman*, an exalted Account of his Merits, and is wrote to create an Opinion in the World, that the *Power of the State* is at prefent employed againft the *Friends of the People*.

The Queftion therefore in this Cafe will be, Whether thofe Men who make thefe Appeals, deferve well of the People to

A 2   whom

whom they appeal? Whether they have done their Country Service or Damage by the Courſe of their boaſted Writings? Whether they had even the Intention of doing Good to the Publick? And whether their pretended Virtues are not real Crimes? Crimes,in the Eye of Reaſon and Conſcience, though neither Laws or Courts of Juſtice ſubſiſted, and though neither had any effect in puniſhing or reſtraining them?

Their partial and inſincere Account of their own Proceedings hath a manifeſt Tendency to create unjuſt Compaſſion in their Behalf, and Reproach againſt thoſe whom they are intereſted to make odious. In detecting the little Arts of their diſingenuous Attempt, I prevent that unrighteous Odium which they have endeavoured to raiſe; and in preventing ſo great a Wrong, I diſcharge the Duty of an honeſt Man.

Summoned by the APPEAL which they have made, and warranted by the neceſſity of a Reply, I may without further Apology or Preface review the Proceedings of the laſt *Five Years*, trace the Steps which have been taken to change the Adminiſtration, and ſhew the conſummate Honeſty of thoſe whoſe Violence hath been employed in this extraordinary Enterprize.

If we turn our Eyes to the Times immediately preceding this bitter and vindictive Strife, Was not all the World at Peace, and the People of *England* happy? Neither Foreign Broils threatned them, nor Domestick Feuds distracted them; they were satisfied with the Powers above them, which gave all just Protection to them. Those who since became the warmeft Men against the Government, were then equally warm for the Government. They affisted their Sovereign with Zeal and Vigor, to punish the Disturbers of his Reign, and the Conspirators against his Title. They thought that all our Enjoyments, as a free and great People, were owing to the Ease and Safety of a Prince, without whom we had been lost and undone. The Mass of the Multitude concurred in the same reasonable Sentiments, and the Crown of *Great Britain* had all that Weight Abroad, which could possibly arise from this happy Situation of our Affairs at Home.

What then was done on the Part of the Government, to alter such a Situation of Affairs? Was any Liberty invaded, any Property injured, or any Man, or Body of Men molested? Was any Grievance or Innovation introduced or countenanced by

the

the Minifters? Was not all poffible Care taken by them, to keep all Men eafy under them? Conftant Attention was given to the Difcharge of our Debts. The yearly Supplies asked of the People were moderate, and the manner of raifing them fcarcely felt. The utmoft Wifdom and Integrity was fhewn in fupplying the Courts of Judicature. Publick Credit could never have better Security, nor was Publick Juftice ever better adminifter'd. The Church of *England*, and all Orders of the Clergy were, as they always ought to be, protected in their Right. All other Religious Perfuafions had the largeft Share of Liberty and Protection: No reafonable Indulgence was ever asked by them, but it was granted to them. The Kingdom was thus in a happy and flourifhing Condition, without Alarms from other Nations, without Divifion among our felves. Liberty was uninvaded, Property facred, and Juftice unfufpected. No Part of the People were either fuffered, or inclined to hurt the reft: All were fafe, and all had Satisfaction.

Could greater Wickednefs be attempted by Man, or greater Mifchief done to the People, than to change this perfect State of Happinefs; to make the People weary of their own Eafe, and diffatisfied with
the

the moſt equal Protection ; to improve all
Accidents againſt the publick Tranquility ;
and whatever threatned the State with Di-
ſturbance, to anticipate all the Evils of it,
by enflaming and diſtracting the People.
In ſhort, to ſow Diſcord in a Nation per-
fectly quiet , and revive Parties when
they begun to be reconciled with each
other ; to make the Burden of Affairs too
heavy a Weight on the Shoulders of the
Adminiſtration; and the Populace ſo
reſtleſs , as hardly to be ruled by the
moſt juſt and reaſonable Meaſures of Government.

When Nations have recovered their Liberties, and ſecured their Conſtitution ;
When the Invaders of their Rights, and
the Enemies of their Country are over-
thrown and defeated : When the Publick
is protected as it ought to be, and the an-
cient Laws appear to be impartially ad-
miniſtered, no Man can ask or deſire more
from the Government of his Country,
than to preſerve and continue theſe Advantages. Whatever new Acceſſions of
Happineſs, whatever Improvement of his
private Affairs may be moſt at his Heart,
the Government can have no particular
Concern in this. Every Addition to his
Fortunes ought to be the Acquiſition of
his honeſt Induſtry; and the Protection of

equal

equal Laws, which he is entitled to, and which he freely enjoys, allows him, in the Purfuit of his private Intereft, all poffible Advantage which can be compatible with the Good of his Country.

The Love of Power, and the Luft of Lucre, as they caufe Defires in Men to ftand above Equality with Mankind; fo they prompt Attempts in enterprizing Minds, incompatible with equal Laws, or publick Good. Ambition and Avarice will not be content with a common Share of Wealth and Authority, nor bound their Defires by the common and honeft Means of indulging them. Thus the Paffions of particular Men interfere with the general Interefts; and urged by the Violence of thofe Paffions, particular Men advance their own Views, even againft the Good of Mankind.

The Generality of the People defire no more than Liberty to exercife their honeft Induftry, and Laws to protect their fair Acquifitions. They feek not after Honour or Power; nor are they fond of thofe Men who happen to enjoy Dftinctions of this Sort. On the contrary, they are apt to be jealous and fufpicious of all who pof-fefs great Wealth, or acquire great Au-thority: Whilft thofe whom Ambition or

A varice

Avarice have taught to envy and covet
thofe glittering Advantages, are conftant
in making Applications to the Jealoufies
and Sufpicions of the Multitude; which
jealous and fufpicious Spirit, if it does
not always appear, yet it is at any time
eafily raifed, and fometimes Accidents
concur to make it more violent. Hence
the Malice and Lufts of bad Men are too
frequently gratified, whofe inceffant Labour it is to make the Great, whom they
envy, be jealoufly treated by the Populace; from thence univerfally odious, and
thereby more eafily undone.

Did the People know how little their
Happinefs is the Purfuit of thofe who fo
eafily draw them into their Quarrels: Did
they know how feldom thofe who are moft
clamorous for the Publick, have any
Meaning at all beyond their private Interefts: Did they fee how eager thofe very
Patriots are to fell them, who are moft
affiduous to court them: Did they fee the
corrupt Applications of thofe who daily
declaim at Corruption, fee Men pretend-
ing that the Treafures of their Country
are lavifhed away by the Adminiftration,
at the fame Time offering *immenfe Sums,*
more than ever were raifed, merely to
outbid the Minifters: Did they confider
that there is not a Meafure of Govern-

B ment,

ment, which thefe Men prefume to defame
as a *dirty Job*, but what they themfelves
would comply with, nay even go beyond
it, could they have the Honour and Favour of being employed in tranfacting it:
Did the People fee the *Malice* and *Selfifhnefs* of thefe publick Spirits, their cruel
Revenge againft all who fet Bounds to
their Schemes of acquiring more Power
than is fafe, and engroffing more Wealth
than is honeft, their unfatisfied Defires
not even content with large Eftates of many Thoufands *per Annum*, but violently
bent to enlarge them, even by any Means:
Did they compare their real Selfifhnefs
with their pretended Difintereftednefs;
their private Paffions againft Particulars,
with their falfe Pretenfion to Zeal for the
Publick: Did they confider that all the
Violence of fuch Men againft Particulars
would, if their Views fhould be at any
Time oppofed by the Publick, turn it felf
with equal Fury againft the Publick; and
that they labour with fo much Induftry to
deftroy the Adminiftration, only becaufe
the Minifters are the Medium and the Bar-
rier between themfelves and the Publick,
which muft become their Prey, when the
Means of Prevention are removed: Did
they fee thefe Things, and that they do
not fee them, is at all Times wholly owing to Neglect or Inattention; They would
never be moved or agitated; carried away

misled by the Arts of Ambition. Aspiring
Men might envy Greatness, and covet
Power, yet neither their Spleen would be
shared, nor their Hopes encouraged by the
People. Mankind would be wiser than
to divide into Parties, and they would
leave those who act only for themselves,
to act altogether by themselves.

That such is the Case very often between the People, and those who profess
themselves Patriots, History and Expe-
rience demonstrate in numberless Instances. Indeed how should it be other-
wise, when Men neither better nor wiser,
but too frequently worse than the rest of
the World, set themselves up as possessed
of all the Wisdom and Goodness left in
the World: When Men who have had
immense Donations, Favours and Bounties
from the Crown, oppose themselves to the
Distribution of Favours by the Crown;
and after having obtained large Instances
of Royal Grace, declaim against the like
Instances to others, as detrimental to the
Publick. In such Cases as these, where
Men would assist all the Schemes and
Measures of the Government, provided
they were favoured with a Share to their
own Wishes in that Government; and
when such Men really have assisted the
Government, whilst their own Views

were

were fatisfied; and ever fince their private Views could not be fatisfied, have oppofed the Government: I fay, In Cafes like thefe, where fuch Men cannot poffibly declaim at any Meafures of Government but what they advifed and approved of, whilft it was their private Intereft to do fo; is it not plain and manifeft that they declaim againft them now, becaufe it is not their private Intereft to approve them? And is fuch an Oppofition as this the Caufe of the People? Or whofe Intereft do thofe Men act for, who act from fuch Motives?

The Struggle between the *Whig* and *Tory* Parties for the Succeffion to the Throne, ended in the Victory gained by the *Whigs*, who fixed that Prince, and that Family on the Throne, whom they had always wifhed to fee there. The Motives of Prudence and Gratitude induced the late King to chufe thofe Men for his Servants, who had been his Friends; and to look upon thofe as his *natural Support*, who had been his *conftant Adherents*. The *Whigs* being thus admitted into Truft, and the *Tories* excluded, the latter became Mutineers againft the Government, becaufe they had no Share in the Government; but their Defigns were not concealed, they complained of their Exclufion

from

from Power as their capital Grievance. And having nothing more alarming than this, the People at length faw the Folly of the Clamour, and in the end grew unconcerned at thofe Complaints, which wholly arofe from *private Interefts.*

The *Tory Faction* thus declining in Credit, and grown unformidable in their Oppofition, the *Whigs* had all the Power and Favour of the Crown to fhare among themfelves; nay, there is a Time ftill recent in memory, I mean when *Layer's Plot* came before the *Britifh Parliament*, at which time there was not a *Whig* in the Houfe of Commons diffenting from the *Body of the Party.*

The *Tory Intereft* grew weak, and the *Whigs* powerful by the Difpofition of Favours and Employments. For if the Profit of ferving the Publick in Places be computed at any Sum, and this be raifed equally upon the People, that Party which is admitted into Truft will have more than a Retribution, whilft the other Party is like a Scale, continually lofing Weight, without any new Acceffion to maintain the Balance; fo that in a certain Procefs of Time the lofing Party muft quite dwindle to nothing, and the prevailing Party, by continuing in Employments of Profit, muft become

come able to purchase all the Lands in the Kingdom.

This had an undoubted Tendency to secure the present Establishment on the most lasting Foundation, as it would most effectually have given the Weight of the *Landed Interest* entirely on the Side of the Government, and have lodged the *natural Power* of the State with those who were *natural Friends* to the present Establishment.

The *whole Body* of the *Whigs* had the highest reason to be satisfied with the Course of Things; but it was impossible to continue that Satisfaction among them long, when once they begun to differ about their several Shares of Power and Favour. It was not difficult to make them agree, that all Employments of Trust and Profit should be divided among themselves: But how to make the respective Allotments, and how to satisfy Particulars that what should fall to their several Shares was as much as properly belonged to them, or that they ought to sollicit no more than what came reasonably to their Shares; this was the difficult Task indeed, and this in the nature of Things must produce Division; so that it was not possible by any means in the World to prevent Faction and Opposition.

Oppofition. Had the Adminiftration been capable of acting with infinite Wifdom and Juftice, yet would this Difagreement of Views and Interefts among their Friends, at all Events, have procured them bitter and implacable Hatred. No *human Abilities* or *Virtues* could poffibly prevent this Diffention; and the Corruption to which it was owing was not in the Miniftry, but in the Heart of Man. Neither was the Conteft which proceeded from it a *Struggle for Liberty*, but a *Contention for Power*, influenced by no *Zeal for the Publick*, but by *private Paffions*; nor conducted for the Good of the People, but altogether for *private Ends*, and for *private Interefts*.

The prefent Adminiftration found every thing eafy at firft, and all their Friends compliant with their Meafures; but it was whilft all their Friends had Expectations, and few or none had met with Difappointments. But when it was found that under this governing Party it would be impoffible to gratify all; when fome had raifed their Hopes too high, and others had rated their Merits higher; when Competitions arofe, and Interefts begun to clafh; when fome imagined that they had a Right to manage all Things, and many defired thofe Things which could not be allowed them, without provoking or difgufting others; then thofe .
who

who had Paffion enough to quarrel about particular Difpofitions, and Pride enough to fancy that they could controul the Management of the whole, begun to form Parties for themfelves, and by all poffible means to break the *Whig Intereft*, which was the governing Party, thereby to introduce their own, and over-rule the reft.

But as thefe *State Schifmaticks* were too few in number to make a Church of themfelves, they had no other way to make themfelves formidable than to fall in with the Views and Attempts of the *Tories*. Neither was this Conceit practicable, but by mutual Engagements to give them a Share of Power and Favour whenever the governing Party fhould be overcome, and thofe who had *long been in* fhould give way to thofe who had *long been out*.

Yet even with this Reinforcement of *Whig Renegadoes*, the *Tory Party* ftill were weighed in the Balance, and ftill were found wanting. What could then be attempted to break the *Whig Intereft?* What was neceffary now to be done, when all the united Squadrons within Doors could make no Stand againft the *Whigs* on the Side of the Adminiftration?

To

To divide the People was then the only Attempt that could do any Service in this Cafe. But what had the People to do in the Quarrels of Parties? Or how were they concerned in the Difpofition of Places? This would weigh very little with the Publick; and the Multitude could never be taught to believe, that the Nation was ever the worfe, becaufe a particular Man had not the Promotion or Employment which he demanded; neither could it by any means make an *honeft* fenfible *Englifhman* uneafy, that one was denied the *Seals*, or another refufed the *Peerage*.

The Bufinefs therefore properly was to perfuade the People that they were ill ufed in general by thofe who had been fo unkind to thefe worthy Gentlemen in particular; fo that making loud Complaints againft publick Affairs became the Confequence of private Ruptures; whilft ambitious Men, not knowing how to make the World intereft themfelves in *petty Quarrels*, nor able to make the Publick adopt *perfonal Refentments*, were pleafed from henceforth to call it a *national Caufe*, and difavowed all Regard to lefs important Concernments.

C

Thus

Thus did they profefs themfelves the Servants of the Publick, that they might make the People their Slaves. In order to get the Publick into their Hands, they laboured to wreft it from the Hands of the Adminiftration. In making themfelves dangerous to the King's Interefts, they meant to make themfelves neceffary to his Service. By the Danger on one Side, and the Neceffity on the other, they hoped and expected that they fhould even compel the Prince on the Throne to the Choice of their own Perfons: And thus by a fatal Election the People of *England* were to become their Poffeffion; we were all to have been at their Mercy, who never regarded us otherwife than as they thought they could fell us. Whilft the Abilities and faithful Behaviour of the Minifters made the Profpect of this more diftant, and the Defign lefs practicable, their Rage was redoubled againft thofe Perfons who gave fuch Obftruction to their Scheme.

To carry on this Scheme more plaufibly, they ftrenuoufly infifted, that they ftill continued to be *Whigs*, notwithftanding that they were governed and led by the worft and moft inveterate of the *Tories*. And though they acted in conjunction with the *Patron of the* SCHISM BILL, yet they

ftill

ftill avowed themfelves zealous Friends to
the *Toleration of the Proteftant Diffenters.*
Nay, though they affociated and concerted
their Affairs with one who had actually
been engaged in the PRETENDER's SER-
VICE, yet they ftill infifted on their invio-
lable Duty to the Prince on the Throne,
and to the *Proteftant Succeffion.*

To enlighten the Underftandings of the
People, it was neceffary next to fet forth
a *Weekly Invective* againft the Adminiftration, to miflead the Ignorant, to inflame
the Weak, and to help the Ill-defigning
with Topicks of Clamour and Uneafinefs.
The Jealoufies and the Sufpicions of the
People were to be applied to, their Paffions
worked upon, and the Multitude made,
every Man of them, as angry as if they had
all of them loft Places, and ftood in the
hopelefs Condition of thofe who made all
this Uproar about it.

To break the *Whig Intereft* more effectually, it was diligently propagated, as a
felf-evident Doctrine, that *Whigs* and
Tories were the fame Men, and had the
fame Meaning; that *Party Names* were idle
Sounds, which had loft their Significations;
and that there was now no other Bufinefs
for *Whigs* or *Tories* than this, that they
fhould all unite *to deftroy the Adminiftra-*

tion. Th*at*

That this might become a popular Undertaking, they fingled out the Perfon of the principal Minifter, and him they devoted to all the Abufe with which they could load his Name; without any regard to his Rank or Diftinction, without any regard to the Character which he had borne among themfelves, without any regard to Truth or Decency, or even common Difcretion. Every Mode of Slander was quite worn out in this Courfe of defaming him, and the vaft Fund of political Scandal quite exhaufted. Not only his perfonal Character was ftretched upon the Rack, but his *private Life* and *Family Affairs* brought before their tremendous Inquifition. Procceding for five Years together in this tedious, unwearied Attempt of making a Minifter odious, under whom the Publick was fafe, and with whom the People were fatisfied, from whom thefe Men had received no Infults to their Perfons, or Attacks upon their Fame, but on the contrary all the Kindnefs and Indulgence that any Minifter could fhew them. more indeed than they could expect, and much more than they could pretend to; infomuch that Strangers, who might take a View of their Conduct, muft think the Cuftom of this Kingdom to be more prodigious than any thing on Earth; They acted as if it was a Maxim

in

in *Britain* to divide the People into angry
Parties whenever any proud ambitious
Man hath a private Quarrel with a Minister; and to change the Adminiſtration it
ſelf, becauſe the imperious haughty Hu-
mour of an aſpiring Malecontent *wills that
it* SHALL *be ſo.*

Such was the wild Riot, the lewd un-
hallowed Licentiouſneſs of Men, who being uneaſy and diſappointed in their private Affairs, carried the Quarrel into publick Proceedings, and endeavoured to in-
ſpire the People with all their *Violence*
without their *Provocations.*

Soon after theſe private Quarrels at
Home had thus occaſioned the forming of
Parties among us, the Affairs of *Europe,*
and the Intereſts of her Kings, which are
always in a State of Fluctuation, ever
prone to change, and often tending to
Diſorder; theſe begun to ſhew an angry
Aſpect, and this encouraged our diſſatiſ-
fied Party to renew their Rage. When
all Men ought in this Caſe of common
Danger, to have united for the Preſerva-
tion of their Country; when the Safety
of all required the Aſſiſtance of all, They
not only denied their own Help, but endeavoured with all their Might, to diſa-
ble thoſe whoſe Duty and Intereſt, and

zealous Care it was to fave and preferve us.

In all our Difputes with Foreign Powers, they conftantly efpoufed the Prince who acted againft us: And when the Crown of *Spain* demanded GIBRALTAR of this Nation, thefe faithful *Englifhmen* took much Pains to fupport thofe Demands; proving as far as they poffibly could carry the falfe Pretenfion, that the SPANIARDS had a Right to the Place; and that a LETTER which *fubjected it to the Power of Parliament*, was a *pofitive Promife* to give it up.

When the only Debate between *Great Britain* and *Spain* was the Affair of GIBRALTAR: When the *Spaniards* declared that they would obferve no Terms of Peace or Friendfhip with us, unlefs we furrendered it to them: When the King, and his Adminiftration, refolutely bent to maintain the Poffeffion, refufed to hearken to thofe Demands, fortified the Place, fupported it againft the Siege, and ftood the Hazard of all Events, rather than lofe it: At that very Time did thefe Men foment a moft unnatural Jealoufy, that the Miniftry fecretly defigned to furrender it: And at the fame Inftant that they themfelves vigoroufly fupported the *Spanifh Claim*

Claim, they charged it as a Crime on the Administration, that they privately favoured that Claim, although the Ministers openly maintained our Poſſeſſion a-ʹ gainſt the *whole Power* of *Spain.*

When the King, and his Adminiſtration, had ſhewed the firmeſt Reſolution in preſerving that important Place: When both Houſes of Parliament had, on the Motion of the Miniſtry, ſolemnly laid before His Majeſty their concurring Reſolutions, declaring their entire Dependance on him, that he would preſerve his undoubted Right to that Place: When his preſent moſt Sacred Majeſty had pledged his Royal Faith to both Houſes, in Anſwer to that Addreſs: Yet did theſe Men proceed even to ſuggeſt, that notwithſtanding this moſt ſolemn Act of the whole Legiſlature, and againſt the Declarations of KING, *Lords* and *Commons*, the Miniſters had by a SECRET ARTICLE, agreed to give up *Gibraltar.*

In Relation to the OSTEND COMPANY, which drew the *Imperial Court* into the Quarrel, they who before that Miſunderſtanding, treated it as Criminal in the Adminiſtration to ſit ſtill, and ſuffer that Company to trade in the *Indies*, even *They* made it criminal in the Miniſters to differ

differ with the *Imperialiſts* about that Company : And what they had inſiſted on as a Duty, became a Miſdemeanor when it was complyed with. We of all Nations, *they ſaid*, ought to prevent Interlopers from running away with our Trade ; and yet preſently after we were taught a new Leſſon : The DUTCH, *they told us*, were the Parties more properly concerned to oppoſe ſuch Interlopers ; and we, *it ſeems*, had little or no Concern in the Caſe.

As all the Princes who had any Miſunſtanding with us, were ſure of their Countenance and good Offices ; ſo whatever Nation continued in Alliance and Friendſhip with us, was the Subject of perpetual Invective. Their fierceſt Rage turned againſt *France*, whilſt the *French* were ſuppoſed to be cordially in our Intereſts. They were continually abuſing and reviling that Court, and their Miniſtry, whilſt they acted in Conjunction with ours. They alarmed the whole Nation about the Repairs of DUNKIRK, in hopes of diſtreſſing our Councils by that Means. They raiſed a Clamour, even that Seven hundred and fifty *Iriſh Recruits* ſhould be deſired by the *French*, whilſt they had Fears that any good Offices on either Side, might contribute to the Harmony between the two Nations. But as ſoon as ever
they

they faw the Scene of Negotiation changed, and that the *French* would be no longer neceſſary or uſeful to the *Britiſh* Intereſts, their Fury againſt the *French* Miniſtry immediately relented, the *Cardinal*
had Peace from that Moment ; and from
thenceforth they never ſo much as aſked
one Queſtion about the *State of Dunkirk,*
becauſe their Clamours againſt the *French*
could have no further Tendency to hurt
the *Britiſh* Adminiſtration.

The GERMANS were their great Fa-
vourites, as long as the *Imperialiſts* were
at Variance with the *Britiſh* Nation. The
Agreement with that Court was mightily
preſſed by them, whilſt they thought it
was impracticable. They repreſented it
as our only *natural Alliance,* as the only
Accommodation that could ſave us from
Ruin. They boaſted it as their *darling
Meaſure.* The Miniſters were moſt in-
ſolently told by a *certain* worthy *Perſon in
Publick,* that *if they would at laſt come into this Meaſure* ; *if they would comply with
thoſe Terms which* HE *had ſo long* DICTA-
TED *to them* ; *why then he would anſwer
for all his Friends, that they would ſupport
the Adminiſtration.* And how did theſe
Gentlemen behave, when the firſt Reports
were ſpread Abroad of this Accommodation? Why, they publiſhed a HAGUE
D   LET-

LETTER, reprefenting this Accommodation as *Perfidious, Scandalous* and *Dangerous*, as a Breach of Treaties, a Compact
that would unite *France* and *Spain* againſt
us; a Project that would involve us in a
bloody and expenſive War; ſo that what
they had preſſed upon the Miniſters as abſolutely neceſſary to ſave us all from
Ruin, when it was comply'd with, was
treated by them, as what would involve
us all in Ruin: What they recommended as
a moſt *natural, prudent,* and *honourable*
Alliance, became, in their Opinions, when
it was concluded, a moſt *perfidious, villai-
nous, dangerous* Meaſure. And thus the
Miniſters were to be made not only odious, if they acted againſt the Advice of
theſe Patriots, but alſo equally odious if
they purſued that Advice. Reſolved and
determined to defame them in every
Shape, they abuſed them for not doing
Things, which when done, they equally
abuſed them for doing; and ſuch Meaſures as could not ſucceed, they made to
be abſolutely neceſſary; yet when theſe
Meaſures were effected, they try'd to
make them as infamous as poſſible.

During the Miſunderſtanding with
SPAIN, the Accidents at Sea furniſhed
them with moſt enflaming Topicks of Invectives, and their Harangues were employed

ployed upon these dreadful Depredations,
'till they had fired the trading Towns
with Clamours againſt the Miniſters.
Though it might be proved, as it hath
appeared on the Examination in Parliament, that all the Depredations ſince the
Ceſſation of Arms preceding the *Peace of
Utrecht*, never amounted, at a *Medium*, to
the Value of *Five Thouſand Pounds* a
Year; which, if it be computed with Relation to the *Jamaica* Trade, hath not
been, in the whole Time of TWENTY
YEARS, *Twenty Shillings per Cent* upon
that Trade; and in Relation to the *private Commerce* carried on with the *Spaniſh
Weſt-Indies*, it hath not amounted to *Two
and a half per Cent*, upon the whole Value of that Trade: Yet as much Noiſe and
Uproar hath been made on this Subject,
as if the whole Trading Intereſt of *Britain*
had been ſacrificed, and all the Merchants
made Bankrupts by theſe Depredations.
At length, when nothing elſe was thought
poſſible to ſatisfy the Clamorous and the
Uneaſy, the King's *Ships of War* at
Jamaica, during this laſt Summer, had
Inſtructions to make Reprizals. And
what then? Why the Merchants would
not conſent to it. They moſt ſtrenuouſly
ſollicited Admiral *Stewart* againſt it; for
that the Deſtruction of the *Trading Ships
of Spain*, would occaſion a ſtop to all

their

their PRIVATE COMMERCE in the *Spanish West-Indies :* And thus ended the fierce Uproar upon that important Affair.

The Administration however have, notwithstanding these inconsistent Clamours of particular Merchants, given fresh Instructions to the same Admiral, that he shall make Reprizals with all possible Vigor. Nor hath their Care been wanting at the *Court of Seville,* where to their Zeal it hath been owing, that the Governors of *Porto Rico* and *San Domingo* have been disgraced, for having countenanced such Depredations on our Commerce. Those Governors have been sent for Home in Irons, to answer the Charge. Strict Orders have been sent to *New Spain* by his *Catholick Majesty,* for the Prevention of these Grievances and Complaints for the future. Commissaries have also been appointed on his Part, to treat with ours, in order to make Satisfaction for all former Losses of this Kind : And as a Beginning of the Reparations which they are to make the *Subjects of Britain,* the *Spanish Court* have already paid a large Sum of Money to the *South Sea Company,* in Retribution of some former Seizures.

Can

Can any Man conceive that all this Hurricane of Oppofition hath not coft the Nation immenfe Sums ; that foreign Princes have not been obftinate in Proportion to the Difficulties and Diftrefs of the Adminiftration at Home; that the Courts Abroad did not perceive that the longer they delayed an Accommodation with us, the more uneafy thefe Patriots would make the People ; and that the Minifters were under the ftronger Neceffity of Peace Abroad, in Proportion to thefe Feuds at Home ? Let any Man who doubts this, read Lord LEXINGTON's Letter from MADRID in the latter Part of the late Queen's Time, where he gives an Account of his Converfation with *King* PHILIP, about the *Catalans. We know,* fays that Prince, *that the Peace is as neceffary to you as it is to us, and that you will not break off the Negotiations for a Trifle.* This was the Language of that Time, and there can be no doubt that the fame Logick hath been made ufe of fince, though there is a moft material Difference between the Neceffity of Peace under the two feveral Adminiftrations. The then Minifters made a Peace neceffary to themfelves, by betraying all the Advantages of a long and glorious War into the Hands of the Common Enemy. The prefent Mini-

ſters

fters found it neceffary, not from any Advantages which they had given to Princes in Enmity with us, but from the reftlefs Strife of Parties at Home, continually working in Favour of thofe Powers againft the Peace and Government of their Country. Is this Patriotifm, this the Caufe of the People? Who can we charge with the Expence of *Additional Troops and extraordinary Supplies*, but thofe who have efpoufed, and even encouraged foreign Courts in their Quarrels with *Britain*? And yet thefe Men call themfelves *Servants of the Publick* —— Perfons who have drawn the Refentments of the Minifters upon themfelves, by the *mighty Good* which they have done to the People.

Whilft they have thus been carrying on this Work of Divifion among the People, it may deferve our Attention to reflect how they have hated the *Prince on the Throne*. No Man can forget their early Profeffions of Duty and Devotion to all the Royal Family. Their Quarrel was, they told us, altogether with the Minifters ; and they have the higheft Senfe of his Majefty's Goodnefs, tho' they had the utmoft Abhorrence of his wicked Miniftry. At his prefent Majefty's Acceffion, they offered up their Vows of Service and Fidelity to the World's End ; they confented to

all

all that could be defired in Behalf of his *Civil Lift*; and were fo very yielding, that, as it has been faid, without any Denial or Contradiction, they offered His Majefty more than He thought good to accept: They would, we are told, have given Him THIRTY THOUSAND Pounds *per Annum*, even out of the SINKING FUND itfelf. But becaufe this very reafonable Propofition had no Countenance, and their Schemes no Credit or Succefs, a formal War muft forthwith be proclaimed with the Throne. The KING muft be libelled in *abufive Parallels*, His *Royal Confort*, without any Regard to the Privilege of her Sex, moft infamoufly infulted and the fame violent Defamation made ufe of againft *Majefty*, as had been fo long and fo liberally thrown out at the Perfons in his Adminiftration.

Had this been all that was attempted againft the Perfon and the Family of our facred Sovereign, nothing could excufe even this, but all muft have treated it as a moft wild and frantick Part, the idle Rage of a Lunatick. But when we faw the fame Malice and Violence, which had appeared under the dark Coverts of libellous Parallels, throw itfelf into a much more formidable Shape, openly invading the ROYAL TITLE to the Crown, difpu-

ting

ting the Terms of Allegiance, ftriking at
the Ties between the Sovereign and Subjects of this Kingdom, denying the Prince
on the Throne the common Supplies for
the Service of the current Year, defaming
indifcriminately all the Meafures of Sixteen
Years paft; afferting, that in all the Ma-
nagements of fo long a Space of Time, there
had not even once been *the leaft Intention
of regarding the Good of the Publick*; and
thus in all things aiming the Blow at
the Foundations of our Happinefs; what
Words can exprefs the Indignation and
Amazement which fuch Proceedings as
thefe muft create in thofe who were Wit-
neffes to them!

Yet whilft they have thought themfelves
at liberty to vilify all Men after this manner, who had either a Share in the Adminiftration, or any Attachment to it, not
fparing even the King and Royal Family,
merely for approving it; hath there at the
fame time been a *corrupt Projector* or a
profcribed Criminal with whom they would
not affociate themfelves, and whom they
have not taken into their moft intimate
Councils? Whoever hath heretofore be-
trayed or fold his Country, hath been entitled to a full Share of their Favour and
Confidence, provided he would but once
come into their Scheme of *deftroying the*
Admi-

Adminiſtration. Nay, the Merits of all ſuch Attempts were ſo conſiderable, that in meer conſideration of this, they undertook to juſtify *B*———'s Character; maintaining the Honour and good Faith of his Dealings, the Integrity of his Heart, and the ſpotleſs Innocence of his Life; whilſt the ſame Hand that had defamed the KING, the *Royal Family,* and *whole Adminiſtration,* became the honeſt, modeſt, and conſiſtent Advocate for *B*———'s *virtuous* Reputation.

It hath often been ecchoed in our Ears, that theſe noble *confederated* Patriots have made a moſt glorious Stand againſt Corruption; I cannot therefore neglect ſome Notice of their great Services in relation to the Bill which was obtained againſt that Practice. They have themſelves in one ſingle Corporation, ſince that Bill paſſed into a Law, ſpent above *Ten Thouſand Pounds* to turn the Election; I mean the Town of *B*——— *d.* In the *City of* LONDON itſelf a very notable Attempt hath lately ſucceeded to improve the *Tory Influence;* and they have taken the Nomination of all *Workmen, Artificers,* &c. from the Court of Aldermen, where the Majority are *Whigs,* transferring this Right of Nomination to the Committee

for

E

for letting the City Lands, where the Majority are *Tories*. I could name number-
lefs Inftances of Profufion and Management in the great Work of *new modelling*
Corporations; but I will not forget that of
L———*le*, where *Fifteen Guineas* a Vote
were given in the Election of a Mayor.
Who then can doubt the Sincerity of our
good Patriots in their Declamations againft
Corruption, or their fincere Defigns in
framing Laws to prevent it?

Thefe, no doubt of it, are Inftances, in
their Apprehenfion, of the great Good
which they have done to the People; and
perhaps they will take it ill of me fhould
I neglect the Wonders which they have
done in defeating Evils and preventing
Grievances which never would have happened. It hath fallen to the Lot of the
prefent Adminiftration, that they have
been obliged to anfwer, not only for things
which they have done, but alfo for Things
which they have not done. Whenever any
dreadful and provoking Chimæra prefent-
ed itfelf to the vifionary Minds of thefe
Men, inftantly the Miniftry were to be as
much abufed and vilified, upon the Suppo-
fition of their making unjuft Attempts, as
if they had actually made them. What is
there that is wicked or monftrous, which
hath

hath not been imputed to their Defigns? And when the Minifters have cleared themfelves from the Imputation, thefe worthy Perfons have ftill pretended to juftify the Sufpicion. *Reftraints of the Prefs* have fometimes been attempted, and there-fore the Adminiftration have been charged with Defigns to obtain fuch a Law. *Acts of Grace* have been fometimes obtained, and therefore the Miniftry are to be char-ged with a View of procuring themfelves this Indemnity. *Members of the Houfe of Commons* have been fometimes EXPELLED for being difagreeable to former Minifters, and therefore the prefent Minifters are to be charged with Defigns to expel whom they do not like. All thefe Accufations have no other Support, than what can be drawn from this notable Reafoning, *that the worft Minifters have made fuch Attempts,* and therefore we are to believe the *worft* of the *prefent Minifters,* though they never fhewed in their Lives any fuch Difpofi-tions, but always acted diametrically op-pofite to them. Nay, though they do this, though they act ever fo uprightly, yet ftill the juft Reward of Integrity is denied them. They are faid to have no good Meaning even in good Actions. They are charged with all the Guilt of bad Defigns, which never were in their Hearts; and

E 2   that

that thofe Defigns which never exifted, have not been attempted, is wholly afcribed to the Difcoveries of thofe who found them out before they had a Being.

Will the *People of England* think that thefe Proceedings are meant for their Good? Or that thofe who carry them on are their Friends? Will they hold and maintain, that all this Outrage and Violence hath no other Source than the Love of their dear Country? Or that it hath no other End than the Happinefs of us, and of our Pofterity? That there is no Ambition or Avarice in this mighty Hunt after Power and Wealth? That there is no Revenge in all this Flame of Paffion? No arbitrary and tyrannical Nature to be feen in fo much lawlefs riotous Uproar? Will the People think that THIRTY THOUSAND Pounds *per Annum* was offered out of the SINKING FUND, purely for their Advantage and Benefit? That Applications and Negotiations were carried on in *Courts* and *Clofets* by thefe *Country Patriots*, merely for the Sakes of their beloved Friends the People? That *Vows of Deftruftion*, SOLEMN LEAGUES *and* COVENANTS, *bloody Affociations*, and *horrid Imprecations*, were made from a Paffion of ferving the Public-

lick

lick, from no private Rancour of Heart, or from no bitter and vindictive Spirit? That Converfations *Eleven Tears* old were trumped up and publifhed for the Good of Mankind, and infamous *private Scandal* vented for the Welfare of the Publick? That Domeftick Life, and the little Affairs of Neighbourhoods, have been drawn into Print for the Service of a Nation? Or that thofe Men who acted in this Manner merit their Affection, or have fhewn them any Marks of Love? Whofe Caufe then have they carried on, but their own *little dirty partial Strife?* Or what Adherents ought they to have, but their *Tools* and *Mercenaries* only?

When they made Alliances with the *Patrons of the Peace of Utrecht*, and put themfelves under the Direction of thofe able Statefmen, did they do this for the Reformation of our Councils, and for the Refinement of our Negotiations? When they took to their Affiftance the *worthy Projector* and *Conductor* of the *South-Sea Scheme*, did they mean by his Advice to *better regulate* the Finances? Did they enter into this Union with the Author of the CANADA EXPEDITION, out of Indignation againft the *Contract* of *Forage?* Or did they make their Peace with the
Author

Author of the *Third and Fourth Subscrip-
tians*, from Abhorrence of the *Bank Contract?* When they entered the Lifts to
plead for *B——*'s Fame, was it meant
for the Good of the Nation? Or had they
the Interefts of the People at Heart, when
they lamented the Spirit of Party, which
kept that juft and upright Man out of the
Adminiftration? Thefe are the Men who
have been the *Servants of the Publick* for
Five Years paft; now let the People judge
themfelves what *Wages* they ought to give,
them.

But fince they have pleaded their *Services to* LIBERTY, as the fhining Merit of
their Oppofition, I will give fome Account of their *Political Creed,* concerning
the *Freedom of the Prefs.* It is, in their
Opinion, an unbounded Licenfe to abufe
all Perfons, and all Things; to blaft the
fair Reputation of any Man; and to af-
perfe the beft Councils of any Miniftry,
without being made accountable for any
Means, right or wrong, which they think
fit to make Ufe of, and without being
obliged to anfwer for the Truth or Juftice, or Equity of their Proceedings. It
is a Liberty to publifh, or if proper Occafion require it, to invent any P R I-
VATE CONVERSATION, however diftant

in

in Time, or scandalous in its Nature, or useless or foreign to the Publick. It is a Liberty to print *Family* and *Domestick* Transactions ; the *Tittle Tattle* of *Neighbourhoods*, and the *Scandal* of *Tea Tables.* It is a Liberty of Writing, without being confined to Truth ; a Liberty of Lying, without being liable to Restraint or Punishment ; and a Liberty of defaming, without being obliged to make Reparation for any Wrong, or Satisfaction for any Injury.

By their Descriptions and Definitions of Liberty, Injuries done to a Nation by Writing are not criminal, nor ought to be accounted for; the Publick hath not the Right of a private Man, and a Minister's Fame is in a worse Condition than that of the meanest Subject; any defamatory Lies may be circulated against him, any odious Designs falsly laid to his Charge. It is honest, great and laudable to destroy his good Name by any Means, merely because he discharges Trusts of a high Nature. He may be abused innocently for what he is innocent of. Justice is to correct all the Members of the Body but the Tongue, all the Instruments of Action but the Pen, and all the Vehicles of Scandal but the Press. No Distinction is to be made
be-

between the Ufe and Abufe of popular
Rights: So that by this Doctrine, Liberty,
like a Sword, is put into Mens Hands, not
only *for Defence*, but even for *Deftruction*;
and whatever Havock is made, wickedly or
wantonly made, it is not to be accounted
for.

Any one, unacquainted with thefe worthy Perfons, would think from their
large Demands of Liberty, and the vaft
Extent to which they ftretch it, that
they make mighty Allowance to other
Men. But they are as narrow in their
Notions on one Side, as they are bound-
lefs and unconfined on the other. Thofe
who fometimes have incurred their
Difpleafure, have occafionally felt the
Weight of Cudgels, even almoft to ASSASI-
NATION. Thofe who have feverely
enquired into their Conduct, and thought
fit to appear againft their Proceedings, have been threatned and menaced
with ANOTHER KIND OF AN-
SWER. When their publick Attempts
have been debated, they have made
Reprizals on the imputed Author, by
attacking his private Circumftances; infomuch that his Drefs, his Air, his
Geftures and perfonal Characterifticks
have been made the Subject of publick
Ridicule; nay, whenever any Pamphlet
or

or Paper hath appeared, which either
provoked their Spleen or their Malice,
they have ufed it as a conftant Pretence
to abufe whomfoever they wanted to re-
vile ; and whether the Perfons attacked
were Authors of the Writings, imputed
to them, or otherwife, they conftantly
reviled and defamed them, as the Authors, in many Cafes too, where they
knew of a Certainty that fuch Perfons
had no manner of Concern in the Writings of which they were accufed ; fo
that Minifters of State, Lords of Parliament, Prelates of the Church, and Members of the Privy Council, have been
treated in this moft infamous Manner,
meerly to gratify the wanton and bafe
Refentment of thofe, who had no other
Way to vent their Rage and Scurrility
againft them, than by abufing them for
Writings which they did not write, and
fometimes never read. The *Chriftianity*
of an *illuftrious Prelate* was drawn into
Queftion, meerly for writing a Defence
of Meafures which they were pleafed to
condemn ; and they evidenced his *Writings for Liberty of Confcience*, as a Proof
that would make his Chriftianity fufpicious.
Monftrous Immorality, and prodigious In-
confiftency, for Men who pretended to affert

F   the

the Rights of Mankind! Whatever Liberty was taken againſt them, hath met with a conſtant Return of all the Violence which they could exert. They have even injured the Liberties of their Country, by overſtraining and abuſing them. They have made the great Privilege of a free Preſs almoſt a common Nuiſance, by their vile Proſtitutions, and their unbounded Licentiouſneſs. To the moſt cruel Defamation, they have conſtantly added the moſt abandoned Scurrility. And when they had laboured for ſo many Years to write out of Doors all Reverence for lawful Government, they wondered how any Man could think that they deſerved to be puniſhed; they appealed to the People as Servants of the Publick, and complained of Proceedings againſt their defamatory Libels, as drawn down upon them by Services done to their Country.

No Man who loves the Liberties or Happineſs of his Country, can delight in Proceedings even againſt Lies and Defamation, which may be equally turned in evil Days againſt the Voice of Truth and Integrity. But as to theſe Men who have wantonly drawn them down on themſelves, Who can they expeQ
ſhould

should pity them? Did those among them who have been Ministers, ever shew the least Regard to the *Liberty of the Press?* Were they even satisfied with the *Common Laws* of the Kingdom? Were they not solicitous, eagerly solicitous for new Restraints? Let these *Friends of the People,* as they call themselves, ask their great Leader, *Lord* B——ke, how indulgent he was to popular Liberty during his Time of Authority? Let us judge from thence, what a tender *Guardian of our Rights* we have lost through that *Spirit of Party* so much complained of, *which hath excluded him from a Share in the Administration:* Let us judge too, how our Rights and Liberties are likely to be protected, should they ever restore him to that share of Power which he so worthily lost. But I fear they will not be so kind as to inform us of the Proceedings against the Press in his Time; nay, I am afraid that they will not admit the Charge, and therefore I am under the greater Necessity to explain it in a particular Manner.

The CRAFTSMAN, in his Paper Nº 4. *Friday, December* 16. 1726. Five

Years

Years ago, when he firſt devoted himſelf a *Servant of the People*, ſet out with this modeſt faithful Account of Lord *B——ke*'s Adminiſtration.

   " I muſt, *ſays he*, do the Perſons
" then in Power the Juſtice to own,
" that they generally ſuffered Writings
" againſt them to be publiſhed with
" Impunity, and contented themſelves
" with applying Argument to Argu-
" ment, and anſwering one Piece of
" Wit and Satire with another. The
" only Inſtances of any Severity which
" we meet with, are burning the Bi-
" ſhop of St. *Aſaph*'s immortal Pre-
" face, and expelling Sir *Richard*
" *Steele* the Houſe of Commons; but
" we meet with no *grievous Impriſon-*
" *ments*, no *expenſive Proſecutions* or
" *burthenſome Fines*, in the Hiſtory of
" that Adminiſtration."

I could not forbear citing this Pa-ragraph, as I am a great Lover of Impartiality, and abhor to ſuppreſs any Part of the *L—— B——ke*'s Praiſe : Having done this, I will now ſhew the Proceedings in *Weſtminſter-Hall*, to puniſh the Writers of thoſe Times,

Times, and the Attempts in the *House of Commons* to reftrain them.

February 1710-11. In the Infancy of that Adminiftration, Mr. *Benfon* having wrote a Letter to Sir *Jacob Bancks*, againft the Doctrine of the *Minehead* Addrefs, *that Kings are accountable to none but God ; and Subjects bound to obey, notwithstanding any Oppression or Tyranny :* A Profecution was ordered againft Him, grounded upon the Pretence of fome free Reflections on the late *Humane* King of *Sweden*'s Clemency to *Count* PATKUL. Vid. *Pol. State of Great Britain*, Vol. I. p. 373.

October 23. 1711. being the Firft Day of *Michaelmas* Term, FOURTEEN *Bookfellers, Printers and Publifhers*, who had then been lately taken up, and committed to the Cuftody of Meffengers by Mr. *Secretary* St. JOHN, for printing and publifhing, appeared at the Bar of the Court of *Queen's-Bench.* Mr. *Darby* was among them, committed only for printing an Account of a Tranflation of that Paffage in *Tacitus*, which relates how *Cefellius Baffus* deceived the Emperor *Nero* with the Promife of an immenfe

menfe, but imaginary Treafure. This, it feems, was interpreted as a Libel upon the then new Project of the *South-Sea Scheme*. Vid. *Pol. State*, Vol. II. p. 388.

On the third of, *December*, 1711, Mrs. *Popping*, a Publisher, was committed to NEWGATE, by a Warrant from Mr. *Secretary* St. JOHN, for publishing a Paper, called the *Proteftant Poft-Boy*, and the Printer thereof was taken into Custody of a Meffenger. *Vid. the fame Vol.* p. 488.

September 4. 1711. *Hurt* the Printer was committed to NEWGATE, by a Warrant from the *Lord Viscount* BOLINGBROKE, for printing and publishing the *Flying-Poft*.

September the eighth following, *George Ridpath* was committed to NEWGATE on the fame Account, by Warrant from the *fame indulgent* Minister. *Vid. Pol. State.* Vol. IV. p. 214.

January the 15. 1712-13, *Baker* the Publisher was fummoned to the *Lord* BOLINGBROKE's Office, on Account of a ludicrous Pamphlet; on which Occafion

fion difcovering that the Author was *Thomas Burnet*, Efq; he was difcharged. But on the 24th of the fome Month, his Lordfhip iffued his Warrant againft Mr. *Burnet*, and obliged him to give Bail for his Appearance at the *Queen's-Bench* Bar. Vid. *Pol. State*, Vol. V. p. 63, 64.

February the 21ft, 1712-13, *George Ridpath* was try'd and convicted at *Guildhall* on the Attorney-General's Information for three Libels, publifhed in the *Flying-Poft*; which Information fet forth, *that a Negotiation of Peace being on Foot, the Defendant, (being a notorious Inventor, and Framer of Libels) did publifh thofe laid in the Information, to ftir up the People to a feditious Diflike of the faid Negotiations.* Vid. the fame *Vol.* p. 155, &c.

April 27. 1713. A Rule of Court being made, that the faid *George Ridpath* fhould appear in the *Queen's-Bench* on the *Firft of May* following; he withdrew from the Violence of that Profecution, and his Recognizances being to the Value of SIX HUNDRED POUNDS, were eftreated, and paid. Vid. *the fame Vol.* p. 377.

May

May 19. following, an Advertiſement was inſerted in the *London Gazette*, ſigned BOLINGBROKE, promiſing a Reward of *One Hundred Pounds*, for the Diſcovering and Apprehending of the ſaid *George Ridpath*.

June 24, 1713. *Hurt* the Printer received Sentence for printing the *Britiſh Ambaſſadreſs's Speech to the French King*, and was adjudged to ſtand *three times in the Pillory*, to pay a *Fine* of 50 *l.* to be *impriſoned for Two Years*, and until he could find ſufficient *Sureties for his good Behaviour during Life*; all which he ſuffered accordingly. Vid. *Pol. State*, Vol. 6. *p.* 79.

Such were the Proceedings of an Adminiſtration, in whoſe Time the CRAFTSMAN tells us that we meet with no *grievous Impriſonments*, no *expenſive Proſecutions* or *burthenſome Fines*. Theſe few Specimens of their Lenity and Indulgence will therefore equally ſerve to ſhew the Mercies *of thoſe Miniſters*, and the Modeſty of the *Craftſman*.

About the latter End of *July*, 1713. Three Meſſengers and a Conſtable ap-
prehended

prehended *Baker* the Publisher by Warrant from the *Secretary of State*, for a Pamphlet concerning the *French Commerce Bill*; but when this *impartial Minister* was convinced that the Author was a *Tory*, he very candidly discharged the Publisher, and dropt the Prosecution. Vide *the same Vol.* p. 118.

A like Instance of his Lordship's excessive Lenity and Moderation may be seen in BEDFORD's Affair. He was prosecuted by the *Whigs* for writing against the *Protestant Succession*, in that well known Book entitled, *The Hereditary Right to the Crown of England asserted.* Part of his Sentence was *to walk round* Westminster-Hall *with a Paper on his Forehead.* His Lordship on this Occasion sent the Queen's Warrant, countersigned by himself, and directed to the Judges of the *Queen's-Bench*, requiring them to spare the *ignominious Part of the Punishment*, in tender regard to his sacred Function, as a Minister of the *Church of England.* Vide *Pol. State*, Vol. 7. p. 167, 362; 462.

DANIEL DE FOE was another Object of his Pity and Mercy. He had only wrote *Three* treasonable *Pamphlets* against

G

gainſt the *Proteſtant Succeſſion*, and in
favour of the *Pretender's Claim*. A private Gentleman (Mr. *Benſon*) thought
the Matter of ſo great Importance, that
he begun a Proſecution againſt him on
the Statute which made it HIGH TREA-
SON to write againſt the Succeſſion. On
this the *Attorney-General* had Orders to
take the Proſecution out of this Gentleman's Hands, under pretence of carrying it on at the Queen's Charge. But
inſtead of proſecuting him on the Statute which made it HIGH TREASON,
he very charitably changed the Indict-
ment into an *Information*, grounded on
the *Common Law*. DANIEL was then
tried, and found guilty; but ſolemnly
profeſſing that he had *no ill Meaning* in
writing againſt the Succeſſion, he was
favoured with the *Queen's Pardon*, and
thought a proper Advocate for the *French
Commerce Bill:* So that his Lordſhip very judiciouſly ſaved him *from the Gal-
lows*, to write in defence of that *uſeful
Project*; which accordingly he did in a
Paper called the MERCATOR.

It will equally ſurprize the World to
read the *Craftſman's* Panegyrick on the
tender Mercies of that Adminiſtration,
and his Complaints againſt the Proceedings

ings of the prefent. Why, the very leaft
Favour *Ld* B—KE fhewed to a Publifher,
who had at any time happened to of-
fend him, was to commit him immediately to NEWGATE. Have any of the
Craftfman's Agents ever fuffered any Severity like this? But had his Lordfhip
confined his Refentment within the
Bounds of *Weftminfter-Hall*, lefs might
have been faid of his Kindnefs to the
Prefs, and his great Indulgence to Authors.

There is no Clamour that hath been
more violently raifed againft the Minifters, or with lefs Truth, than the Defign of *reftraining the Prefs by Act of
Parliament*; a Defign which they always abhorred, and moft folemnly difavowed, and which they have never attempted in any Shape, or by any Means.
But what will the World fay, if they
find thefe very Men who have afperfed
the Miniftry *falfely* with this odious Defign, attempting this Reftraint themfelves, and labouring it with all their
Might, during their Time of Power?
This let the *Journals of both Houfes* te-
ftify for our more certain Information.

Janu-

January 17. 1711-12, (as I obferved in another Point very early in the Adminiftration). Mr. *Secretary* St. JOHN delivered to the Houfe of Commons a Meffage from the QUEEN, under the *Royal Sign Manual*, the Eighth Paragraph of which was this:

ANNE REG.

HER Majefty finds it neceffary to obferve, how great Licenfe is taken in publifhing falfe and fcandalous Libels, fuch as are a Reproach to any Government. This Evil feems to be grown too ftrong for the Laws now in Force. It is therefore recommended to you to find a Remedy equal to the Mifchief.

St. James's, Jan. 17, 1711.

Upon the reading this Meffage, it was among other Things refolved, *That this Houfe will take the moft effectual Courfe to put a ftop to the publifhing thofe falfe and dangerous Libels, which have expofed her Majefty's Government to Danger and Reproach.*

The next Day Sir *Gilbert Dolben* reported to the Houfe, the Addrefs drawn up in Anfwer to her Majefty's Meffage; which Addrefs concludes in this remarkable Manner. " We

" We are very fenfible how much the
" Liberty of the Prefs is abufed, by
" turning it into fuch a Licentioufnefs
" as is a juft Reproach to the Nation;
" fince not only Falfe and Scandalous
" Libels are printed and publifhed a-
" gainft your Majefty's Government,
" but the *moft horrid Blafphemies* againft
" GOD and *Religion*. And we beg Leave
" humbly to affure your Majefty, that
" we will do our utmoft to find a Reme-
" dy equal to this Mifchief, and that
" may effectually cure it.

The fame Meffage was fent to the
Lords; but in their Addrefs to the
Queen, they very wifely took no Notice
of the Matter.

The next Step was to go into a *Com-
mittee* on that *gracious* Part of the
Queen's Meffage thus brought into the
Houfe of Commons by Mr. *Secretary* St.
JOHN.

Accordingly *June* the third, 1712.
Sir *Gilbert Dolben* reported from that
Committee, the Refolutions which had
been taken, and they were as follows.

RESOLVED,

1. " That the great Liberty taken
" in printing and publishing false, scan-
" dalous and impious Libels, creates
" Divisions among her Majesty's Sub-
" jects, tends to the Disturbance of the
" Publick Peace, to the Increase of Im-
" morality, Profaneness, and Irreli-
" gion, and is highly prejudicial to her
" Majesty, and her Government.

2. " That the want of a due Regula-
" tion of the Press is a great Occasion of
" this Mischief.

3. " That all Printing Presses be re-
" gistred with the Names of the Own-
" ers, and their Places of Abode.

4. " That to every Book, Pamphlet
" and Paper, which shall be printed,
" there shall be set the Name, and Place
" of Abode of the Author, Printer and
" Publisher thereof.

5. ". That no Bookseller, or other
" Person, shall sell or disperse any Book,
" Pamphlet or Paper, to which the
" Name, and Place of Abode of the
" Author, Printer and Publisher, shall
" not be set.

Those

Thofe Refolutions were read, and agreed to, and a BILL was ordered to be brought in purfuant to the fame.

To the matchlefs Honour of the fame *Houfe of Commons* I muft alfo remember, that on the 11th *Day* of *April* they voted the *Memorial of the States General*, in Vindication of themfelves from a Cenfure paffed on their Conduct, to be a *pretended Memorial*, as alfo a *falfe, fcandalous, and malicious Libel*; for which they ordered Mr. BUCKLEY, who tranflated and printed it, into the Cuftody of the *Serjeant at Arms* attending their Houfe.

In the Month of *June*, an *Order of Council* was made at *Kenfington*, offering a Reward of *Fifty Pounds* for difcovering the *Printers* and *Publifhers* of the Reafons, which *Twenty Four* of the Lords had entered on the Journals of their Houfe againft the PEACE OF UTRECHT; fo that the then Miniftry would not even fuffer the *common Protefts* to be printed.

On *Tuefday* the 10th of *June*, the *Houfe of Commons* read a *firft time* the Bill *for reftraining the great Licentioufnefs of the Prefs*, and ordered it to be read a fecond time.

After

After which they voted the BISHOP *of*
ST. ASAPH's *immortal Preface* malicious
and factious, ordering that it fhould be
burnt by the *common Hangman*; which
was done accordingly.

The Bufinefs of Parliament being put
an End to on the 21ft of *June*, the laudable Project of *reftraining the Prefs*
dropt for that Year ; but it was too
much at the Hearts of its Patrons to be
quite laid afide.

April 9, 1713, the Parliament again
affembled, and to convince the World
that the *Reftraint of the Prefs* was neither
to be deferred nor forgot, the QUEEN
in her *Speech* was advifed to exprefs her
felf thus :

" Several Matters were laid before
" you laft Seffion, which the Weight
" and Multiplicity of other Bufinefs
" would not allow you to perfect ; I
" hope you will take a proper Oppor-
" tunity to give them due Confidera-
" tion.

" I cannot however but exprefly men-
" tion my Difpleafure at the unparal-
" lelled Licentioufnefs in publifhing fe-
" ditious and fcandalous Libels.
" The

" The Impunity fuch Practices have
" met with, encourage the Blafphem-
" ing every thing Sacred, and the
" Overthrow of all Religion and Go-
" vernment.

" Profecutions have been ordered;
" but it will require fome new Law to
" put a ftop to this growing Evil, and
" your beft Endeavours in your refpe-
" ctive Stations to difcourage it."

The Lords with the fame good Senfe
as before, avoided making any Anfwer
in their Addrefs to this Part of the
Speech.

But the COMMONS, *April* 18th.
Ordered a BILL to be brought in, *to*
prevent the Printing and Publifhing of
blafphemous, treafonable, feditious and
fcandalous Libels, and for the better Re-
gulation of the Prefs.

What now was the Confequence of
all this laborious Enterprize to reftrain
the Prefs? Why after *Lord* B———KE
and his Collegues in Power had done all
that they could, had engaged the
QUEEN in preffing this Point for two

H   Sef-

Seffions fucceffively, and had perfuaded the *Houfe of Commons* to order in *two feveral Bills* for that Purpofe : Their own Party mutiny'd againft them, and their own Friends obliged them to give it up. In the End an Expedient was agreed upon ; they refer'd the Bill to a *Committee of Supply*, where it being taken into Confideration, they impofed the *Duty on all printed Papers* ; and this they hoped would ferve to *reftrain the Prefs* in fome Meafure, by loading it with a new Charge. So that the TAX which we pay at this Inftant for STAMPS on all *fingle Sheets and Half-Sheets* of Paper, this *very Tax* is the Effect of *Lord B——ke's* Zeal againft the *Liberty of the Prefs*, and every *Stamp* impreffed on our Papers, is a *Memorial of his Labours to take away that Privilege.*

Nor was this Reftraint a fufficient Satisfaction to the then Miniftry ; but the QUEEN by their Advice almoft directly *reproached* both Houfes of Parliament with having defeated Her *gracious Intentions to reftrain the Liberty of the Prefs.* Thus Her Majefty exprefsed Herfelf in Her Speech to Parliament, *March* 2. 1713-14. *I wifh,* faid She, *that effectual Care had been taken as I*
have

have often defir'd, to fupprefs thofe feditious Papers *and factious Rumours, by
which defigning Men have been able to fink
Credit, and the Innocent have fuffer'd.* So
we fee·that this *Reftraint of the Prefs* was
the conftant View of thofe Minifters,
from the Beginning to the End of their
Time of Power. There was fcarcely a
Seffion, there was hardly one Speech
from the Throne but what was employ-
to this Purpofe. And yet what makes
the Matter more aftonifhing, is that
thefe very Minifters *begun the Work of
Abufe,* carried it on in the moft *outra-
geous* Manner, and countenanced more
Licentioufnefs on their own fide, than ever
had been known in the Kingdom.

I had not been fo particular in this
Detail of thofe Meafures, if thofe Men
who clamour againft the prefent Government for proceeding againft Libels, had
not fet them the *ftrongeft* Examples in
every fhape, for punifhing and reftraining all fuch Writings; fome Examples
indeed which they never were inclined,
and I am affured never will be prevail'd
on to follow. God forbid that the prefent Adminiftration fhould purfue any
fuch wicked Scheme of reftraining the
Prefs; nor am I fond of recommending

Pains

Pains and *Penalties* againft any Man; but when thefe Men complain of Punifhments which arife only from the *known* Laws of their Country, they Clamour againft that very Ufage which they have inflicted upon other Men, and declaim at Proceedings which they continually made ufe of whilft they were in Power, and had the Laws on their fide. Is it not monftrous that *B——* fhould cenfure Profecutions againft *his own Libels*, who profecuted all the Writers againft him *as Libellers*; and that he fhould appeal againft the ordinary courfe of Juftice, who not only proceeded againft his Adverfaries in that way, but even in the *Houfe of Commons* procuring MEMBERS to be expell'd for having wrote *againft his Meafures*: And not content even with thefe Severities, endeavoured with all his might to obtain a TOTAL RESTRAINT OF PRINTING, by propofing that all *Preffes* fhould be *regifter'd*, as alfo that all *Writers*, *Printers* and *Publifhers* fhould be obliged to publifh their *Names* and *Places* of *Abode.* Had this worthy Scheme taken Place, what a bleffed Situation would this *Servant of the People* have found himfelf in on his removal from the Adminiftration? And how uneafy would

his

his Condition have been as a *Libeller
againſt this Miniſtry?* He muſt have
expoſed himſelf *perſonally* to the Power
of rigorous Laws, and have ſet his
Name to *all his Invectives* againſt thoſe
Perſons *whom he hath libelled.*

Let me ask at the ſame Time, what
hath this *preſent Miniſtry* done in the
courſe of a *ten Years Adminiſtration* to
prejudice the Freedom of the Preſs, or
to leave the Liberties of their Country
in a worſe Condition than they found
them? Proſecutions grounded on the
common Law have been the only ones attempted, and thoſe but ſeldom, nor
directed at all but on great Provocation ;
nor hath any Paper been proceeded
againſt as a *Libel* but what was really
wicked and *immoral* in itſelf ; nor hath
any Violence been uſed in Trials of this
nature, nor any but *fair* and *impartial*
Juries returned, nor any Method made
uſe of to *byaſs* and *corrupt* them ; no
Puniſhments againſt *Libellers* have been
carried on out of the ordinary courſe of
Juſtice. Have any Applications been
made to Parliament, any Reſtraints on
the Preſs recommended *from the Throne,*
any *Bills* brought in, any *Reſolutions*
taken, or even moved for againſt the Preſs ?
No,

Lightning Source UK Ltd.
Milton Keynes UK
UKOW02f2359030516

273519UK00001B/41/P